Contents

Introduction   2

Brief History of Riddles   3

Math Riddles   4

Answers   39

Introduction

Mathematics - the quintessential universal language of numbers, patterns, and logical reasoning. While many see math as a dry academic subject, this book aims to reveal its delightfully puzzling side through a kaleidoscope of ingenious math riddles.

Welcome to the mind-bending world of Math Riddles for Kids and Adults. Within these pages lies a meticulously curated treasury of over 100 devilishly clever numerical and logical conundrums. From disarmingly simple warm-up brainteasers to advanced riddles that will challenge even seasoned puzzlers, this book is a comprehensive mental workout using mathematics as its playing field.

Whether you're a parent looking to make math fun for your children, a teacher seeking fresh ways to engage students, or simply a math enthusiast who revels in cerebral challenges, this book promises hours of head-scratching satisfaction. The riddles cut across a wide array of mathematical concepts like arithmetic, algebra, geometry, sequences, probability, and more.

But make no mistake - these aren't just textbook math problems regurgitated in riddle form. Each puzzle represents a unique marriage of mathematics and creative reasoning, often spiced with clever wordplay, lateral thinking challenges, and "aha!" moments guaranteed to electrify your gray matter.

Expertly sequenced to gradually ramp up complexity, the book allows both kids and adults to start on a confident footing before delving into increasingly intricate territory. Whether tackled solo or enjoyed as a group activity, solving these riddles unlocks the profound pleasure of cracking a code through math.

So steel your mental faculties, study the clues scrupulously, and get ready to embrace math mastery through the joy of riddling. The game is afoot - let the cogs in your mind begin whirring!

Riddles

Riddles have been around for millennia, dating back to ancient civilizations like Sumer, Egypt, and Greece. They were used not just for entertainment, but also as a way to test wisdom, intelligence, and wit. In many cultures, the ability to solve complex riddles was seen as a mark of great mental acuity.

At their core, riddles are puzzling statements or questions that require creative, lateral thinking to decipher their veiled meanings. This exercise in abstract reasoning and unconventional problem-solving stimulates various regions of the brain responsible for language, logic, creativity, and cognitive flexibility.

Solving riddles engages the brain's executive functions, including working memory, cognitive control, and task switching. As you juggle different interpretations and lines of thought, your brain's neural pathways strengthen, enhancing skills like focus, analysis, and information processing.

Moreover, riddles often rely on verbal and linguistic gymnastics, wordplay, and double meanings. Unraveling these linguistic knots bolsters language comprehension abilities while igniting imagination and divergent thinking. The "aha!" moments upon cracking a riddle release rewarding bursts of dopamine, reinforcing curiosity and motivation.

In our fast-paced world overloaded with information, regularly exercising your brain with riddles helps build vital cognitive reserves and mental resilience. So whether you're a curious child or an inquisitive adult, indulging in these ancient brain teasers can be a fun, enriching way to keep your mind agile, creative, and sharp as a whip.

Math Riddles

1. If the sum of the digits of a two-digit number is 9, and the number obtained by reversing the digits is 36 less than the original number, what is the original number?

2. Two numbers are such that their sum is twice their product. If one of the numbers is 3, what is the other number?

3. A number is six times the sum of its digits. If the number is decreased by 36, the digits are reversed. What is the number?

Math Riddles

4. Three numbers are in geometric progression, and their product is 216. If the sum of the first and third numbers is 18, what is the second number?

5. A number consists of two digits whose sum is 9. If 18 is added to the number, the digits are reversed. What is the original number?

6. The sum of three consecutive even numbers is 42. What is the smallest of these numbers?

Math Riddles

7. I am a function of angles, bounded between -1 and 1, with a unique relationship to circles. What am I?

8. A person has a certain number of coins that are either quarters or dimes. The total value of the coins is $4.35, and there are 27 coins in total. How many quarters does the person have?

9. In a certain year, the sum of the ages of a father and his son was 60. Six years later, the product of their ages was 784. What were their ages in the original year?

Math Riddles

10. A baker has a certain number of identical cupcakes to sell. If he sells them in packages of 6, he will have 2 cupcakes left over. If he sells them in packages of 8, he will have 4 cupcakes left over. What is the smallest possible number of cupcakes the baker has?

11. Three numbers are in arithmetic progression, and their product is 720. If the sum of the first and third numbers is 22, what is the second number?

12. A train travels at a certain speed for 2 hours, then at three times that speed for 1 hour, and then at twice the original speed for another hour. If the total distance traveled is 180 miles, what was the original speed of the train?

Math Riddles

13. A rectangle has an area of 96 square inches. If the length is increased by 4 inches and the width is decreased by 2 inches, the area remains unchanged. What are the original dimensions of the rectangle?

14. A certain number consists of two digits whose sum is 12. If the number is tripled and then 36 is subtracted from the result, the digits are reversed. What is the original number?

15. In a group of 120 people, 2/3 of the people have taken mathematics, and 3/4 of the people have taken science. If 45 people have taken both subjects, how many people have taken neither subject?

Math Riddles

16. A rectangle has an area of 144 square inches. If the length is doubled and the width is halved, the area remains unchanged. What are the original dimensions of the rectangle?

17. A certain number consists of three digits with the property that the sum of the first and last digits is twice the middle digit. If the digits are reversed, the new number is 63 more than the original number. What is the original number?

18. A bag contains an equal number of red, green, and blue marbles. If there are 24 marbles in total, and the ratio of red marbles to green marbles is 3:2, how many blue marbles are in the bag?

Math Riddles

19. A rectangular swimming pool has an area of 720 square feet. If the length is increased by 4 feet and the width is decreased by 2 feet, the area remains unchanged. What are the original dimensions of the pool?

20. A certain number consists of two digits whose sum is 13. If the digits are reversed and the resulting number is subtracted from the original number, the answer is 45. What is the original number?

21. A bookshelf contains novels and biographies. If 2/5 of the books are novels, and there are 18 more biographies than novels, how many books are on the bookshelf if there are 54 biographies?

Math Riddles

22. A rectangular garden has an area of 120 square meters. If the length is increased by 2 meters and the width is decreased by 1 meter, the area remains unchanged. What are the original dimensions of the garden?

23. A certain number consists of three digits with the property that the sum of the first and last digits is equal to the middle digit. If the digits are reversed, the new number is 297 less than the original number. What is the original number?

24. A bag contains an equal number of red, green, and blue marbles. If there are 30 marbles in total, and the ratio of red marbles to blue marbles is 5:3, how many green marbles are in the bag?

Math Riddles

25. A rectangular field has an area of 1,440 square yards. If the length is increased by 8 yards and the width is decreased by 4 yards, the area remains unchanged. What are the original dimensions of the field?

26. A certain number consists of two digits whose sum is 11. If the digits are reversed and the resulting number is added to the original number, the answer is 132. What is the original number?

27. A bookshelf contains novels and biographies. If 3/7 of the books are novels, and there are 12 more biographies than novels, how many books are on the bookshelf if there are 42 novels?

Math Riddles

28. A rectangular garden has an area of 180 square meters. If the length is increased by 3 meters and the width is decreased by 2 meters, the area remains unchanged. What are the original dimensions of the garden?

29. A certain number consists of three digits with the property that the sum of the first and last digits is three times the middle digit. If the digits are reversed, the new number is 297 more than the original number. What is the original number?

30. A bag contains an equal number of red, green, and blue marbles. If there are 36 marbles in total, and the ratio of red marbles to green marbles is 2:3, how many blue marbles are in the bag?

Math Riddles

31. A rectangular field has an area of 2,400 square yards. If the length is increased by 10 yards and the width is decreased by 6 yards, the area remains unchanged. What are the original dimensions of the field?

32. A certain number consists of two digits whose sum is 15. If the digits are reversed and the resulting number is subtracted from the original number, the answer is 63. What is the original number?

33. A bookshelf contains novels and biographies. If 5/9 of the books are novels, and there are 24 more biographies than novels, how many books are on the bookshelf if there are 60 biographies?

Math Riddles

34. A rectangular garden has an area of 240 square meters. If the length is increased by 4 meters and the width is decreased by 3 meters, the area remains unchanged. What are the original dimensions of the garden?

35. A certain number consists of three digits with the property that the sum of the first and last digits is four times the middle digit. If the digits are reversed, the new number is 342 less than the original number. What is the original number?

36. A bag contains an equal number of red, green, and blue marbles. If there are 42 marbles in total, and the ratio of red marbles to blue marbles is 7:5, how many green marbles are in the bag?

Math Riddles

37. A certain number consists of two digits whose sum is 13. If the digits are reversed and the resulting number is added to the original number, the answer is 176. What is the original number?

38. In a bookstore, the price of a notebook is two-thirds the price of a pen. If the total cost of 4 pens and 3 notebooks is $31.50, what is the cost of 2 pens and 5 notebooks?

39. Three numbers are in geometric progression. The sum of the first and third numbers is 20, and the sum of the second and third numbers is 45. What is the second number?

Math Riddles

40. A seller buys articles at $12 each and sells them at $16 each. What is the minimum number of articles the seller must sell to make a profit of at least $100?

41. Two positive integers have a sum of 50 and a product of 560. If one integer is greater than the other by 6, find the two integers.

42. A worker can do a job alone in 12 days. After working alone for 4 days, he is joined by another worker, and they finished the job in 4 more days. How many days would the second worker take to do the job alone?

Math Riddles

43. A train travels at a certain constant speed for 3 hours, after which it travels at twice that speed for 2 more hours. If the total distance traveled is 300 miles, what is the original speed of the train?

44. In a mixture of milk and water, the ratio of milk to water is 5:3. If 12 liters of the mixture are taken away and replaced with water, the new ratio of milk to water becomes 5:4. How many liters of milk were there originally in the mixture?

45. A rectangular swimming pool has a length that is 8 meters more than twice its width. If the area of the pool is 120 square meters, what are the dimensions of the pool?

Math Riddles

46. Three friends decide to split the cost of a meal. The first friend pays 1/4 of the total cost, the second friend pays 1/3 of the remaining cost, and the third friend pays the remaining $21. If the total cost of the meal is $60, how much did the second friend pay?

47. A merchant has 120 kg of rice to sell. He sells one-third of his stock at 10% profit and the remaining at 20% profit. If he earned a total profit of $40, what was the cost price per kg?

48. In a circle with radius 6 units, a chord is drawn that is 8 units long and 4 units away from the center of the circle. What is the area of the shaded region between the chord and the arc of the circle?

Math Riddles

49. A cylindrical tank has a base radius of 2 meters and a height of 5 meters. If the tank is filled with water at a rate of 0.3 cubic meters per minute, how long will it take to fill the tank?

50. In a bag, there are 4 red balls, 5 green balls, and 3 blue balls. Two balls are drawn at random from the bag. What is the probability that they are of different colors?

51. A bakery sells three types of pastries: donuts, muffins, and croissants. The numbers of donuts, muffins, and croissants sold on Monday were in the ratio 2:3:5. If the bakery sold a total of 220 pastries that day, how many croissants did it sell?

Math Riddles

WELL DONE YOU ARE HALFWAY THROUGH!

Math Riddles

52. Three numbers are in arithmetic progression, and their product is 3,024. If the sum of the smallest and largest numbers is 38, what is the middle number?

53. A boat travels 20 km upstream in a river in 4 hours and travels the same distance downstream in 2 hours. If the speed of the boat in still water is 6 km/h, what is the speed of the river's current?

54. In a circle with radius 10 units, a chord is drawn that is 12 units long and 6 units away from the center of the circle. What is the area of the shaded region between the chord and the arc of the circle?

Math Riddles

55. A cylindrical tank has a base radius of 3 meters and a height of 8 meters. If the tank is filled with water at a rate of 0.4 cubic meters per minute, how long will it take to fill the tank?

56. In a bag, there are 5 red balls, 6 green balls, and 4 blue balls. Three balls are drawn at random from the bag. What is the probability that they are all of the same color?

57. A video rental store rents out three types of movies: action, comedy, and drama. On a particular day, the numbers of action, comedy, and drama movies rented were in the ratio 5:7:3. If the store rented out a total of 150 movies that day, how many comedy movies did it rent out?

Math Riddles

58. Three numbers are in geometric progression, and their sum is 98. If the smallest number is 6, what is the largest number?

59. A train travels 180 km at a certain constant speed. If the train had traveled at twice that speed, it would have taken 2 hours less to complete the journey. What is the actual time taken by the train to travel the 180 km?

60. In a circle with radius 8 units, a chord is drawn that is 10 units long and 5 units away from the center of the circle. What is the area of the shaded region between the chord and the arc of the circle?

Math Riddles

61. A cylindrical tank has a base radius of 4 meters and a height of 7 meters. If the tank is filled with water at a rate of 0.5 cubic meters per minute, how long will it take to fill the tank?

62. In a bag, there are 6 red balls, 7 green balls, and 5 blue balls. Four balls are drawn at random from the bag. What is the probability that at least two of them are green?

63. A bakery sells four types of pastries: donuts, muffins, croissants, and scones. The numbers of donuts, muffins, croissants, and scones sold on Tuesday were in the ratio 3:4:5:2. If the bakery sold a total of 280 pastries that day, how many scones did it sell?

Math Riddles

64. Four numbers are in geometric progression, and their product is 16,384. If the sum of the smallest and largest numbers is 34, what is the second number?

65. A boat travels 30 km upstream in a river in 5 hours and travels the same distance downstream in 3 hours. If the speed of the boat in still water is 8 km/h, what is the speed of the river's current?

66. In a circle with radius 12 units, a chord is drawn that is 16 units long and 8 units away from the center of the circle. What is the area of the shaded region between the chord and the arc of the circle?

Math Riddles

67. A cylindrical tank has a base radius of 5 meters and a height of 9 meters. If the tank is filled with water at a rate of 0.6 cubic meters per minute, how long will it take to fill the tank?

68. In a bag, there are 7 red balls, 8 green balls, and 6 blue balls. Five balls are drawn at random from the bag. What is the probability that at least three of them are green?

69. A video rental store rents out four types of movies: action, comedy, drama, and sci-fi. On a particular day, the numbers of action, comedy, drama, and sci-fi movies rented were in the ratio 3:5:4:2. If the store rented out a total of 280 movies that day, how many sci-fi movies did it rent out?

Math Riddles

70. Three numbers are in arithmetic progression, and their sum is 42. If the largest number is 20, what is the product of the three numbers?

71. A train travels 240 km at a certain constant speed. If the train had traveled at 75% of that speed, it would have taken 2 hours more to complete the journey. What is the actual time taken by the train to travel the 240 km?

72. In a circle with radius 10 units, two chords are drawn such that they intersect at a point 6 units away from the center of the circle. If one chord is 12 units long and the other is 8 units long, what is the area of the quadrilateral formed by the two chords and the arcs of the circle?

Math Riddles

73. A cone and a hemisphere have equal base radii of 6 cm. If the total surface area of the cone and hemisphere is 112π square cm, what is the height of the cone?

74. Six friends decide to play a game where each person contributes some money to a pot. The second person contributes twice as much as the first, the third contributes three times as much as the first, and so on up to the sixth person. If the total amount in the pot is $120, how much did the first person contribute?

75. In a circle with radius 12 units, two chords are drawn such that they intersect at a point 8 units away from the center of the circle. If one chord is 14 units long and the other is 10 units long, what is the area of the quadrilateral formed by the two chords and the arcs of the circle?

Math Riddles

76. A spherical balloon has a surface area of 36π square inches. A cube is inscribed inside the balloon such that each of its vertices touches the inner surface of the balloon. What is the volume of the cube?

77. A company manufactures two types of products, X and Y. The profit margins for X and Y are 25% and 30%, respectively. If the company sells 100 units of X and 200 units of Y, and makes a total profit of $9,000, what is the cost price of one unit of X?

78. In a circle with radius 8 units, two chords are drawn such that they intersect at a point 4 units away from the center of the circle. If one chord is 10 units long and the other is 6 units long, what is the area of the quadrilateral formed by the two chords and the arcs of the circle?

Math Riddles

79. A solid metal sphere has a radius of 6 cm. A cylindrical hole of radius 2 cm is drilled through the center of the sphere. What is the remaining volume of the sphere?

80. A retailer marks up the cost price of an item by 30% and then offers a 20% discount on the marked price. If the final selling price of the item is $96, what is the cost price of the item?

81. In a circle with radius 10 units, two chords are drawn such that they intersect at a point 6 units away from the center of the circle. If one chord is 12 units long and the other is 8 units long, what is the area of the quadrilateral formed by the two chords and the arcs of the circle?

Math Riddles

82. A solid metal cone has a base radius of 4 cm and a height of 9 cm. A cylindrical hole of radius 2 cm is drilled through the center of the cone parallel to its base. What is the remaining volume of the cone?

83. A company manufactures three types of products, X, Y, and Z. The profit margins for X, Y, and Z are 20%, 25%, and 30%, respectively. If the company sells 150 units of X, 200 units of Y, and 100 units of Z, and makes a total profit of $18,000, what is the cost price of one unit of Y?

84. In a circle with radius 12 units, two chords are drawn such that they intersect at a point 8 units away from the center of the circle. If one chord is 14 units long and the other is 10 units long, what is the area of the quadrilateral formed by the two chords and the arcs of the circle?

Math Riddles

85. A solid metal pyramid has a square base with side length 6 cm and a height of 10 cm. A cylindrical hole of radius 2 cm is drilled through the center of the pyramid parallel to its base. What is the remaining volume of the pyramid?

86. A retailer marks up the cost price of an item by 40% and then offers a 25% discount on the marked price. If the final selling price of the item is $108, what is the cost price of the item?

87. In a circle with radius 10 units, two chords are drawn such that they intersect at a point 6 units away from the center of the circle. If one chord is 12 units long and the other is 8 units long, what is the area of the quadrilateral formed by the two chords and the arcs of the circle?

Math Riddles

88. A solid metal cube has an edge length of 8 cm. A cylindrical hole of radius 2 cm is drilled through the center of the cube parallel to one of its edges. What is the remaining volume of the cube?

89. A company manufactures four types of products, X, Y, Z, and W. The profit margins for X, Y, Z, and W are 20%, 25%, 30%, and 35%, respectively. If the company sells 100 units of X, 150 units of Y, 200 units of Z, and 50 units of W, and makes a total profit of $24,000, what is the cost price of one unit of Z?

90. In a circle with radius 12 units, two chords are drawn such that they intersect at a point 8 units away from the center of the circle. If one chord is 14 units long and the other is 10 units long, what is the area of the quadrilateral formed by the two chords and the arcs of the circle?

Math Riddles

91. A solid metal cylinder has a base radius of 5 cm and a height of 10 cm. A cylindrical hole of radius 2 cm is drilled through the center of the cylinder parallel to its base. What is the remaining volume of the cylinder?

92. A retailer marks up the cost price of an item by 50% and then offers a 30% discount on the marked price. If the final selling price of the item is $119, what is the cost price of the item?

93. In a circle with radius 8 units, two chords are drawn such that they intersect at a point 4 units away from the center of the circle. If one chord is 10 units long and the other is 6 units long, what is the area of the quadrilateral formed by the two chords and the arcs of the circle?

Math Riddles

94. A solid metal sphere has a radius of 8 cm. A cylindrical hole of radius 3 cm is drilled through the center of the sphere. What is the remaining volume of the sphere?

95. A company manufactures five types of products, X, Y, Z, W, and V. The profit margins for X, Y, Z, W, and V are 20%, 25%, 30%, 35%, and 40%, respectively. If the company sells 100 units of X, 150 units of Y, 200 units of Z, 50 units of W, and 75 units of V, and makes a total profit of $30,000, what is the cost price of one unit of W?

96. A circle is inscribed in a square of side length 12 cm. Another circle is inscribed in the first circle. If the area of the region between the two circles is 36π square cm, what is the radius of the smaller circle?

Math Riddles

97. A solid metal cone has a base radius of 6 cm and a height of 12 cm. A cylindrical hole of radius 3 cm is drilled through the center of the cone parallel to its base. What is the remaining volume of the cone?

98. A retailer bought some items for $2,000 and marked up their price by 60%. After selling a few items, the retailer decided to offer a 30% discount on the remaining items. If the final revenue from selling all the items was $3,360, what was the number of items that were sold before the discount was offered?

99. In a circle with radius 10 units, two chords are drawn such that they intersect at a point 6 units away from the center of the circle. If one chord is 12 units long and the other is 8 units long, what is the area of the region enclosed by the two chords and the arcs of the circle?

Math Riddles

100. "Three mathematicians, Alice, Bob, and Charlie, are discussing their ages. Alice says, 'If you multiply my age by Bob's age and then add Charlie's age, you get 245.' Bob then says, 'If you multiply my age by Charlie's age and then subtract Alice's age, you get 112.' Lastly, Charlie says, 'If you multiply my age by Alice's age and then subtract Bob's age, you get 132.' Can you figure out the ages of Alice, Bob, and Charlie?"

Answers

1. 63

2. 6

3. 45

4. 6

5. 63

6. 12

7. The cosine function.

8. 15 quarters

9. Father was 48, son was 12

10. 28 cupcakes

Answers

11. 10

12. 20 miles per hour

13. Length = 12 inches, Width = 8 inches

14. 84

15. 20 people

16. Length = 12 inches, Width = 12 inches

17. 495

18. 6 blue marbles

19. Length = 30 feet, Width = 24 feet

20. 86

Answers

21. 90 books

22. Length = 12 meters, Width = 10 meters

23. 594

24. 6 green marbles

25. Length = 40 yards, Width = 36 yards

26. 65

27. 84 books

28. Length = 15 meters, Width = 12 meters

29. 369

30. 12 blue marbles

Answers

31. Length = 50 yards, Width = 48 yards

32. 90

33. 108 books

34. Length = 16 meters, Width = 15 meters

35. 621

36. 10 green marbles

37. 89

38. $22.50

39. 15

40. 25 articles

Answers

41. 16 and 34

42. 18 days

43. 40 miles per hour

44. 50 liters

45. Length = 20 meters, Width = 6 meters

46. $13

47. $2 per kg

48. 12 square units

49. 35 minutes

50. 17/36

Answers

51. 100 croissants

52. 14

53. 2 km/h

54. 36 square units

55. 50 minutes

56. 1/15

57. 70 comedy movies

58. 49

59. 6 hours

60. 20 square units

Answers

61. 44 minutes

62. 91/136

63. 40 scones

64. 4

65. 2 km/h

66. 64 square units

67. 60 minutes

68. 143/323

69. 40 sci-fi movies

70. 480

Answers

71. 8 hours

72. 48 square units

73. 12 cm

74. $5

75. 72 square units

76. 27 cubic inches

77. $40

78. 24 square units

79. $224\pi/3$ cubic cm

80. $80

Answers

81. 48 square units

82. $56\pi/3$ cubic cm

83. $40

84. 72 square units

85. 120 cubic cm

86. $90

87. 48 square units

88. 448 cubic cm

89. $40

90. 72 square units

Answers

91. 235π cubic cm

92. $100

93. 24 square units

94. 448π/3 cubic cm

95. $40

96. 4 cm

97. 108π cubic cm

98. 20 items

99. 72 square units

100. Alice is 5 years old, Bob is 7 years old, and Charlie is 35 years old.

Printed in Great Britain
by Amazon